GOOD MORNING, LORD

Devotions for Young Mothers

MARY FOXWELL LOEKS

BAKER BOOK HOUSE

Grand Rapids, Michigan

The following publishers have given permission to quote Scripture references from their copyrighted material:

Berk.   — The Modern Language Bible, The Berkeley Version © 1959, 1969 by Zondervan Publishing House, Grand Rapids, Michigan.

RSV   — The Revised Standard Version, © 1946, 1952, 1971, 1973 by the Division of Christian Education of the National Council of the Churches of Christ in the United States of America.

Phillips — The New Testament in Modern English translated by J. B. Phillips, © 1958, 1960, 1972 by J. B. Phillips.

NEB   — The New English Bible, © 1961, 1970 by The Delegates of the Oxford University Press and The Syndics of the Cambridge University Press.

NIV   — The New International Version, © 1973 New York Bible Society International, by the Zondervan Corporation, Grand Rapids, Michigan.

LB   — The Living Bible, © 1971 by Tyndale House Publishers, Wheaton, Illinois.

To

KRISTIN and EMILY

"Mommy, Emily, and Kristin take a walk."
by Kristin, age 4

1. NO-STRINGS-ATTACHED KIND OF LOVE

Scripture Reading: I Corinthians 13 (Phillips)

"... the greatest of these is love" I Cor. 13:13b.

In a recent column, Ann Landers asked her readers, "If you had it to do over again, would you have children?" An overwhelming 70 percent of those readers who responded said "NO."

For myself, I would unhesitantly say that the joys of being a parent far outweigh the hardships. I have a hard time understanding why so many responded as they did, unless their motivation for becoming a parent in the first place was wrong. Even though there are many rewards in parenting, a person should never become a parent simply for those rewards. The motivation must be, "I have something of myself to give, a special, no-strings-attached kind of love, and I can best give it by being a parent."

The Greeks used the word *agapé* for this kind of love—"willing another's highest good." It's the kind of love God is, and demonstrates. Paul, in I Corinthians 13 gives us a beautiful definition of it.

Every time I read this chapter, I am slapped in the face with how far short I really come. So I submit my "amplified version" of I Cor. 13:1-8 not as a description of what I've attained, but rather as a goal toward which I'm working. This is not intended to be a substitute for the actual text; please read the Scripture along with my words.

* * *

5

Though I speak with the tongues of Haim Ginott and Dr. Spock, and have not God's kind of love, the sound of my words has as much value as a dripping faucet, or a squeaking oven door.

If, because of my age and experience, my knowledge exceeds that of my children; but I do not in love recognize that sometimes they must experience and discover things by themselves, that knowledge is worth nothing. If I had that faith which can move mountains, and tried to force it on my children in an unloving way, it would amount to nothing.

If I give up that new dress so my son can have the football equipment that means so much to him; even if I were to give my own life to save my child's life, and did it without God's kind of love, I would achieve precisely nothing.

This love of which I speak is slow to lose patience —even when asked, "Mom, why—?" for the seventeenth time that day. It looks for a way of being constructive—if my child brings home a spelling paper with every word wrong, I can praise him for the care with which he printed his name in the corner, and, one at a time, we'll work together at learning to spell those words. Love is not possessive; even when my child chooses to confide in an adult other than myself. Love doesn't allow me to be anxious to impress friends and acquaintances with the athletic prowess or academic achievements of my children. Nor does love permit cherishing an unrealistic picture of my children.

Love has good manners; even when no one's home but the children. Love is not touchy; even after a very short night. Love does not keep account of evil; "Is that that naughty Timmy Smith who trampled all over my flowers last Spring?" Love doesn't gloat over the wickedness of other people's children: "My Kristin would never do a thing like that!"

Love knows no limit to its endurance; even if a daughter has been sick, cleaned up, and put back to bed four times already that night. Love knows no end to its trust; that diary is private, even if the key is accessible. Love knows no fading of its hope; even after the last ballot from the Student Council election is tallied, and my son's opponent has won; there's always next year! God's kind of love can outlast anything. It is, in fact, the one thing that still stands when all else has fallen.

2. MARVELOUS IS THY WORKMANSHIP

Scripture Reading: Psalm 139

"Thou didst possess my inward parts and didst weave me in my mother's womb. I praise Thee because I have been fearfully and wonderfully made; marvelous is Thy workmanship, as my soul is well aware. My bones were not hidden from Thee when I was made in secrecy and intricately fashioned in utter seclusion. Thine eyes beheld my unformed substance, and in Thy book all was recorded and prepared day by day, when as yet none of them had being" Ps. 139:13-16, Berk.

I lie here, holding close the child that only yesterday was living and growing within me. Today I can count her fingers and toes, marveling at their paper-thin nails! Today I can stroke the dark, newborn hair on her head. I am amazed that God knows the number of those hairs!

For nine months, He was busy "weaving" this child together in my womb. Each day He performed new miracles within me, all according to His master plan. He didn't forget a single detail.

During those nine months I spent a little time worrying—I'm ashamed about that now—and I spent a fair amount of time just plain being curious. Now I look at this perfect little girl, and with David I want to shout, "Marvelous is Thy workmanship!"

3. A COUPLE OF TUNA SANDWICHES

Scripture Reading: John 6:1-13

"And the King will answer them, 'Truly I say to you, as you did it to one of the least of these my brethren, you did it to me'" Matt. 25:40, RSV.

They were just a couple of tuna sandwiches in a brown paper sack. Not any different from the hundreds of lunches I've put up before. Knowing how it is with young teen-aged boys, I figured that on a beautiful afternoon, with no school to go to, a snack might come in handy.

Just thinking about what happened to that lunch gives me chills down my back! My Andy took off after a crowd of people who were following that man, Jesus. They all were hoping He might do some more miracles. He took them on quite a hike, clear over to the other side of the sea of Galilee. Before anybody realized it, it was suppertime. As it turned out, not one person in that whole crowd (except my Andy) had thought to bring any food! Andy heard Jesus' disciples talking; they were wondering how to feed everybody. Now don't get me wrong—Andy's a good kid—but I was really surprised when he told me he gave his lunch to the disciple Andrew, to give to Jesus. It would have been much more like him to have slipped behind a tree and eaten it himself; fourteen-year-old boys are all stomach, it seems sometimes. I wouldn't believe what happened next, except I know Andy wouldn't lie to me. Jesus took those two tuna fish sandwiches, and fed the *whole crowd*—5000 men, plus women and children! And after they'd all had enough to eat, there were twelve baskets *left over!* Imagine that!

They were just a couple of tuna sandwiches in a brown paper sack. And making a bag lunch is just one of the dozens of routine jobs in a mother's day. I never thought of it as actually doing something for Jesus!

4. A CHARGE TO PARENTS

Scripture Reading: Deuteronomy 6:1-9

"Hear, O Israel, the Lord our God is one Lord, and you shall love the Lord your God with all your heart, with all your soul, and with all your strength. These words with which I am now charging you shall be

*written on your heart; and you shall impress them
deeply upon your children. You shall talk of them
when you are sitting at home, while you walk on the
road, when you lie down, and when you get up"*
                              Deut. 6:4-7, Berk.

God has given parents a sacred responsibility. We
are responsible for teaching our children to love God.
This is not something that can be relegated entirely
to the Sunday school teacher. For, although the church
can certainly be of some help, teaching children to
love God is not primarily the job of the church.

First of all, God's truths are to be part of us. "These
words . . . shall be written on your heart." We cannot neglect the study of God's Word ourselves and
expect to "impress [it] deeply upon [our] children."
And our teachings are not to be isolated from the
routines and responsibilities of our daily lives. Our
children need to see that God's Word is practical.

Talk of God's truths when you are taking a walk
around the block, and when you are driving a daughter home from a piano lesson.

Talk of God's truths when you tuck your children
in at night, and when you get up, and as you sit
around the breakfast table.

Let your children know what God has taught you,
and let them know that Christianity is real to you.

Let your actions reinforce the words you say.

I believe Christianity was meant to be a part of my
walking, talking, working, eating, sleeping, and playing tennis. It was meant to be part of a neighborhood
coffee, a conference with my son's teacher, and a Fri-
day night date with my husband. I don't mean that
I always talk about God, or about being a Christian
at all those times. I don't even consciously think about

God, or about being a Christian at all those times. But that doesn't alter the fact that I am God's child, and that relationship cannot be put in the closet, as though it were a suit of Sunday clothes.

God's truth, and our relationship to Him, is relevant to our "sitting, walking, lying down, and getting up."

5. BE STILL...

Scripture Reading: Psalm 46

"Be still and know that I am God; I will be exalted among the nations, I will be exalted on the earth. The Lord of hosts is with us" Ps. 46:10, 11a, Berk.

Be still
When the car won't start, and you only have fifteen minutes to get there.
Be still
When the last quart of milk is spilled on the floor you just washed.
Be still
When you discover that the living room sofa has been newly decorated with blue magic marker.
Be still
When the refrigerator, filled with food for all that company, breaks down.
Be still
When your husband finally arrives, but the dinner was ready and the children clamoring to eat 45 minutes ago.

11

Be still
When your son comes home from his first fist fight bloody and bruised.
Be still
When the chocolate-covered good-by kiss gets on your new beige jacket that is "dry clean only."
Be still
When the baby's sick, and you can't go to that luncheon.
Be still
When there's only one swing, and three little girls want to swing on it.
Be still
When the washing machine quits, and you haven't a clean diaper in the house.
Be still!

Being still doesn't mean you don't take appropriate action when that action is possible. You can be still with your hands or feet moving rapidly. Being still, for a busy mother, is usually more of an inner posture than an outer one. It is a quiet trust in a personal God, and a confidence that He will be exalted.

6. JESUS LOVES ME!

Scripture Reading: Romans 8:31-39

"For I am convinced that neither death nor life, neither angels, nor demons, neither the present nor the future, nor any powers, neither height nor depth, nor anything else in all creation, will be able to separate us from the love of God that is in Christ Jesus our Lord" Rom. 8:38-39, NIV.

One of the great hymns of the faith (in my judgment) is written off by almost everybody over age ten as being "for little kids." It is, indeed, "for little kids," but it also carries a powerful message for people of every age. Even for mothers! It is hard—maybe impossible—to convince your child that Jesus loves him, if you haven't first gotten hold of the fact that Jesus loves *you*. Does that fact seem hard to grab hold of today? "The Bible tells me so," concludes this little hymn. Let the Bible tell you so! Read the latter part of Romans 8.

I know Jesus loves me, but I sometimes get busy stewing about a particular problem, and forget that His love is there. Sometimes I even savor my misery to the extent that I don't want to let the love of Jesus put my problem in its proper perspective. What a wretched substitute for Jesus' love this is! I want to sing, as I teach my children to sing.

> "Yes, JESUS loves me,
> Yes, Jesus LOVES me,
> Yes, Jesus loves ME!
> The Bible tells me so.

I want to allow the power of this truth to affect my life. Today.

7. EYE COMMUNICATION

Scripture Reading: Psalm 32

"I will instruct thee and teach thee in the way which thou shalt go: I will guide thee with mine eye"

Ps. 32:8.

When I was a college student, I was once the guest of a family who had two rambunctious little boys. What impressed me as I sat at their table was the very clear eye communication that took place without a word being spoken. A few years later, when I was teaching school, I found out for myself how effective eye communication can sometimes be.

What makes for good eye communication? Why does it work between some people, and not between others? An obvious first requirement is good eyes—eyes that see. The other requirement, I think, is a good, working, trusting relationship. This kind of relationship builds the sensitivity necessary to know when to look up to receive the message. Eye communication usually doesn't work well between two people who are strangers.

The apostle Peter had this kind of relationship with Jesus. He denied knowing Jesus three times, as had been foretold. Then Peter looked up, and as he did so, his eyes met those of Jesus (Luke 22:60-62). That one bit of eye communication produced bitter tears and real repentance in Peter. Peter was a different man after this experience. Yet that look would have meant nothing to a blind man; and it meant nothing to the other onlookers who had no real relationship with Jesus.

When children don't respond to eye communication, we as parents have to resort to verbal, and other more forceful, means of communication. God treats His children in much the same way. Only His children can be guided with His eye—those outside the family are either blind or not sensitive enough to look in His direction. The psalmist warns us not to be as the horse or the mule, whose temper must be curbed by bit and bridle (Ps. 32:9). God won't have to resort to the bit and bridle so often with us if we are sensitive to His eye communication.

Today, ask God to make you responsive to Him, so He can "guide you with His eye." And try some "eye communication" with your children, especially if you are a mother who tends to overuse verbal communication.

8. GOD'S WATER SPRINKLER

Scripture Reading: Psalm 100

"He veils the sky in clouds and prepares rain for the earth: he clothes the hills with grass and green plants for the use of man" Ps. 147:8, NEB.

After several weeks of hot, sunny days, we woke this morning to find it was finally raining. Kristin remarked, "Mommy, God turned on His water sprinkler!"

I must admit that there are times when rain depresses me—especially when the skies are gray for long periods at a time—but today the rain is a blessing. God's "water sprinkler" falls on everybody's yard and garden, whether the owners be good or bad. God's "water sprinkler" doesn't run up the water bill. It cools the air; it nourishes the ground. In its abundance, it is a metaphor of God's mercy.

Today, as I watch and listen from my porch, the rain provides gentle accompaniment for my Psalm of Praise: "For the Lord is good; his mercy is everlasting; and his truth endureth to all generations" Ps. 100:5. Even as God's rain will be available for my

15

children's generation, so will God's mercy and truth be available. That fact merits praise!

> "Make a joyful noise unto the Lord, *Mother*. Serve the Lord with gladness: come before his presence with singing" Ps. 100:1, 2.

9. TIED DOWN

Scripture Reading: Acts 16:16-40

"In view of that charge, he threw them into the inner prison and fastened their feet in the stocks. But about midnight Paul and Silas were worshipping as they sang hymns to God..." Acts 16:24, 25, Berk.

Have you ever felt tied down? Stuck at home with only a couple of small children for company? I know I've felt that way. I have a prescription for those kinds of days. It comes from Paul and Silas.

Paul and Silas were tied down. Literally. In a place not nearly as pleasant as your home or mine. Their feet were locked in stocks, and they were confined in a prison which was probably dark and damp. They may well have had cockroaches and rats for company. In addition, Paul and Silas had just been severely beaten. Despite their predicament, at midnight, Paul and Silas were heard singing hymns!

Prescription to be taken when feeling tied down: Sing a hymn of praise. Out loud. In front of your children—they won't mind if you flat a little. If necessary, repeat dosage.

I have tried this, and it does work! My focus shifts from myself and my problems to God.

The praises of Paul and Silas got results; God performed a series of miracles which significantly altered their circumstances. God doesn't always respond to our praise by altering our circumstances; but our praise usually results in an altering of our attitude, and improves our ability to cope with whatever circumstances we face.

NOTE: If you don't have a hymnal and haven't memorized a lot of hymns, I recommend *Hymns,* published by InterVarsity Press.

10. WHAT IS THAT IN YOUR HAND?

Scripture Reading: Exodus 4:1-20

"The Lord said to him: What is that in your hand?" Exod. 4:2a, Berk.

What is that in my hand? My first inclination is to protest and say, Lord, I don't have anything that could possibly do You any good. There's nothing in my hand worthy of an offering to You. But then I remember Moses—all he had in his hand was a stick. Nothing exceptional about it at all until Moses yielded it to God, and then "took *God's* staff in his hand." With it, God enabled Moses to perform some of the most terrible and powerful miracles in all of Scripture.

All David had in his hand was a sling and a few stones. All Gideon had was a "handful" of men. All Dorcas had in her hand was a needle and thread. All Peter had was his fishing net. I'm so glad God uses ordinary things! A stick, a sling, a needle, a net—

these were ordinary things put at God's disposal which accomplished tremendous results.

What is that in my hand? What is that in your hand? Maybe it's a box of stationery and a pen. Maybe it's a pair of knitting needles. Maybe it's a telephone or a washing machine. Or some home-made cookies. Or a piano. Or an income-tax refund check. Or a paintbrush. Dare to put that which is in your hand, no matter how inconsequential it may seem to you, in God's hand!

> Take my life, and let it be consecrated, Lord, to Thee.
> Take my moments and my days; Let them flow in ceaseless praise.
> Take my hands, and let them move at the impulse of Thy love.
> Take my feet, and let them be swift and beautiful for Thee.
> Take my voice, and let me sing, Always, only for my King.
> Take my lips, and let them be filled with messages from Thee.

> —Frances R. Havergal

11. IS _____ TOO HARD FOR THE LORD?

Scripture Reading: Genesis 17:15—18:19

"Is any thing too hard for the Lord?" Gen. 18:14a.
"For nothing is ever impossible with God" Luke 1:37, Berk.

Is _____ too hard for the Lord? You fill in the blank

with whatever seemingly impossible circumstance faces you today. You think your situation is really impossible? Read about Sarah's, in Genesis 17 and 18. God told Abraham that he, at age 100, would have a son —and Abraham laughed. Sarah, overhearing the announcement that she would conceive a son, laughed. Impossible! She was 90 years old, and had long ceased menstruating. Sarah received a mild rebuke when the Lord asked Abraham, "Why did Sarah laugh? Why does she question whether she can bear a child? Is anything too hard for the Lord?"

Sarah's initial skepticism must have been overcome, and she must have put her faith in the Lord. For in due time, Isaac, the promised son, was born to her. God proved Himself able to cope with the impossible. Many years later, the writer of the Hebrews commends Sarah in the well known "Faith chapter."

> "By faith Sarah personally received potency for conception and that when past the normal age, because she regarded the Promiser trustworthy. And so from one person, and he already impotent, there were born descendants as the stars of heaven in numbers and countless as the sand on the seashore"
> Heb. 11:11-12, Berk.

You left your wallet somewhere up at the shopping center? The clerk at the store where you shopped said it would be impossible for her to help you? You have an impossible number of things to do before this weekend? Michael has been an impossible child lately? . . . A line from a chorus I learned when I was in elementary school comes to mind: "God specializes in things that seem impossible. . . ."

The same God who proved trustworthy to Sarah stands ready to prove Himself trustworthy to you.

12. LETTING GO

Scripture Reading: Exodus 1:20—2:10

"She tucked the child in [the basket] and set it among the reeds near the riverbank" Exod. 2:3b, Berk.

From the moment of birth, when the doctor clamps the umbilical cord, it is clear that being a parent involves "letting go." But how much should one let go? How much freedom should we give? How soon? I don't think there are any easy answers, because each child and each circumstance is different.

Moses' mother had to "let go" of her son in a most dramatic fashion. As soon as she knew she had given birth to a boy, she knew that giving him up was inevitable. The Pharaoh had cruelly commanded that all male Hebrew infants be destroyed.

Two things strike me about Moses' mother. First, she was very careful in her preparations (Exod. 2:3), and, second, her actions seem to show a real trust in God. F. B. Meyer, in *Through the Bible Day by Day*, says of her: "There was no fear of fatal consequences, only the quiet expectancy that God would do something worthy of Himself."

I haven't had to let a child go away to kindergarten yet, much less to college. And there is time yet before I need to think about letting a daughter go to become someone's wife. But learning to let go begins long before any of these significant occasions. One very early freedom we found we had to give was that of access to the basement staircase. Like Moses' mother, we tried to make careful preparations. We carpeted the stairs, closed in the open stairwell, and put a soft pad at the bottom. Then, for several weeks, we practiced going up and down with Emily, at first moving her hands and feet, then just being close behind as she learned to move them herself. Finally one day Kristin yelled, "Emily's coming downstairs by herself." I held my breath, and let her go.

All this probably sounds absurdly over-protective to anyone who hasn't been around a year-old baby lately. (Take a good look at the next one you see.) I think, however, that the principle of making careful preparations prior to giving our children "a longer leash" applies, regardless of the age of the child.

Today, ask yourself, is there an area in which I should be giving my child more freedom? In what way can I prepare him, myself, and the surroundings so my child can handle this freedom?

13. LETTING GO — A SEQUEL

Scripture Reading: Genesis 2:11-22

And [Moses] looked this way and that way, and when he saw that there was no man, he slew the Egyptian, and hid him in the sand" Exod. 2:12.

Despite our very careful preparations and trust in God, there are times when our children do fall. There are times when they do make wrong choices. Here, in spite of the fact that Moses' mother so carefully nurtured him in his early years, and in spite of her trust in God, Moses made a very wrong choice. The immediate consequences were that his people, the Hebrews, rejected him, and he was put on Pharaoh's

21

"wanted" list. To Moses' mother, his future must have looked bleak indeed.

The times when our children fall and make wrong choices are perhaps a parent's most painful times. But I think two things can be said. First, God surely can empathize with parents in such situations. He made every possible preparation for Adam and Eve short of actually making their choice for them; and still, they made the wrong one. Second, the end of the story may not be in sight yet! In chapter 2 of Exodus, it looks as though Moses is finished—but the rest of the book goes on to tell how God did use Moses in an exciting and powerful way.

Memorize Proverbs 3:5-6 today. Perhaps you could do it as a family. If you already know the King James Version, try memorizing it in another version.

14. O TASTE AND SEE

Scripture Reading: Psalm 34

"O taste and see that the Lord is good; blessed is the man who trusts in Him" Ps. 34:8, Berk.

It is not my intent to alter Scripture; but I don't think it does injustice to the psalmist's thought to suggest that we taste, see, touch, hear, and smell that the Lord is good! Each of our senses is a gift from God; each of them can uniquely demonstrate our God's goodness.

For a time after Emily's birth, the doctors were concerned that she wasn't seeing properly. The ophthalmologist told me there was nothing to do except wait three months, and test her eyes again. Not being a very good waiter, I decided I would at least do everything possible to develop Emily's other senses. So we listened to music. We took "touch tours" through the house, when I would run her hands over as many different textures as I could find—window glass, wooden shutters, various fabrics, concrete, ice, etc. When in the kitchen, we would investigate smells—cinnamon, nutmeg, even garlic!

I believe God can give us a heightened appreciation for the ordinary things around us if we try to see things through our children's eyes, or smell through their noses! I know that has been true for me. Sixteen-month-old Emily "discovered" leaves the other day. As she walked, then jumped, through the piles of leaves, experiencing their delicious sounds, textures, and colors for the first time, I looked up into the blue sky, felt the warm sun on my face, and couldn't help but exclaim inside myself, "God, you're good."

Today, lick a beater, and share one with your child! As you experience God's good gifts with your children, remind them (and yourself) that "every good gift is from above."

15. ON MOTHERS-IN-LAW

Scripture Reading: Ruth 1, 2

"Do not urge me to desert you by turning away from you; because wherever you go, there will I go; wherever you lodge I will lodge. Your people are my people, and your God, my God" Ruth 1:16, Berk.

One of the best known daughter/mother-in-law relationships in all of literature is pictured in the Book of Ruth. It is true that Ruth and Naomi lived in a day and culture quite different from ours. But their relationship was a very good one, so perhaps by studying it we can find some principles that apply to our relationships with our own mothers-in-law.

The development of Ruth's relationship required sacrifice. She had to leave her native country, her friends, and her remaining family. For us, the circumstances will be different, but a worthwhile mother-in-law relationship will cost us something. At the very least, it will cost us time, energy, and sometimes the putting aside of our pride.

Another thing that impresses me about Ruth and Naomi is that they were able to take help and advice from each other. I remember coming home from grocery shopping to be told by my baby-sitter, "Your mother-in-law is in cleaning up Kristin and Emily's room." Instead of being appreciative, I was embarrassed and defensive. "She doesn't think I'm doing a good enough job . . . She could at least have told me she was coming . . . She doesn't realize that within 24 hours, that room'll look just like it did before she came. . . ." These were some of the thoughts I had! Receiving help graciously is not always an easy thing to do!

Ruth said, "Do not urge me to desert you by turning away from you." There is more than one way to turn away. We can live in the same town, and "turn away" by cutting off the lines of communication between ourselves and our mothers-in-law. Ruth did not turn away. She kept the lines of communication open.

Ruth had a deeply rooted faith in, and loyalty to,

God. This relationship with God affected her relationship with her mother-in-law. If we are rightly related to God, His love in us will enrich, and in some cases, heal, our other relationships.

16. PASS THE SALT, PLEASE

Scripture Reading: Matthew 5:13; Colossians 4:6

"You are the salt of the earth ..." Matt. 5:13a, RSV.

Did you ever try eating scrambled eggs without salt? Or popcorn? Or any one of the thousands of foods we customarily put salt on?

Jesus said those who believed in Him were to be as salt. In the New Testament times, in addition to enhancing flavor, salt was frequently used as a preservative for foods. We need to ask ourselves the question, "What things can I do to enhance the flavor of, and preserve, the good things around me?" As mothers, we have a unique opportunity to pass God's truth on to our children, and thus preserve it. In a day when much is being written about the disintegration and demise of the family, we who believe that the family has been instituted by God can help to preserve it.

Paul reminds us that our speech should be always gracious, "seasoned with salt" (Col. 4:6). Our speech can preserve and enhance, or it can destroy. Enhancing the flavor of the lives around us can be done in all sorts of ways—even by something as simple as telling our children stories of things that happened during our childhoods.

Are you being salt? Or have you unnecessarily put those around you on a low-salt diet?

17. ON BEING CONTENT

Scripture Reading: Philippians 4:11-13; I Timothy 6:5-8; Hebrews 13:5

"I have learned to make ends meet in whatever situation I am. I know how to live simply and I know how to relish plenty; I am acquainted with all of it in every way, to be filled up and to be hungry, to enjoy abundance and to suffer privation" Phil. 4:11, 12, Berk.

Being discontent is a disease which is no respecter of age, sex, or economic bracket. The media bombard and titillate our senses with things that glitter, shine, whiten, taste delicious, or entertain. Things that, if we could simply acquire them, would surely answer all our problems. Yet some of the most discontented people I know are the ones who have acquired vast numbers of possessions. I can see the seeds of discontent even in my own family. My two-year-old with one cookie in her mouth, and one in her hand would like "one more cookie, Mommy." My four-year-old would like a "Dressy Bessy"—just like on T.V. And Mom? She wouldn't mind having a piano.

If we ask God to help us to be content, will God respond by allowing us just the bare essentials of bread, water, and a roof over our heads? "When we have nourishment and covering, let us be content with these" (I Tim. 6:8, Berk.). Of course not! Our God is far more generous than the most generous of human parents. He *delights* in giving good gifts to His children (James 1:17).

Does being content mean we are obliged to feel guilty if God provides us with that new house, or steak for dinner? Paul says, "I know how to live simply, and I know how to relish plenty...." If God, in His goodness, supplies with plenty, let's be generous with it, but, like Paul, let's relish it!

The point is, our contentment shouldn't be based on what things we have or haven't; or what things our neighbors have or haven't. It should be based on the fact that we have Christ Himself!

> "Let what there is, suffice, for He has said, 'I will never give you up, nor ever at all desert you'"
> Heb. 13:5, Berk.

I think a realization of what that verse means is surely a cure for discontent.

18. A LETTER AT THE DEATH OF A BABY BOY

Scripture Reading: Revelation 21:1-7

"I shall be God to him, and to Me he shall be a son"
Rev. 21:7, Berk.

Dear Karen,

I'm feeling some of the hurt with you, as the reality that your little boy is gone begins to take hold. There's a lump in my throat, too, as I realize you won't be able to see him grow up—you won't have the joys and griefs of mothering him.

27

But I got to thinking a little about what's ahead, for him! Can you imagine—he'll be taking his first steps on the streets of Heaven! Hannah was a mother who certainly knows how special a little boy is. Perhaps she'll be the one who'll let him hold her finger as he takes those first staggering steps. And maybe she'll be the one who will coax him into taking his first steps alone! Perhaps Dorcas will see to it that his hems get let out, and that the buttons are sewn on for that growing boy of yours. And Joshua! Just think what it would be like for a little boy to climb into his lap, and hear—first hand—about the battle of Jericho! . . . Maybe Peter will take him fishing some day.

Karen, he's not ever going to fall out of a tree and break his leg—for there's no pain or tears there! He won't ever be afraid of the dark—for there's no darkness there. The King of Kings, the Lord of Lords, He's the very one who said, "Let the little children come to me." I expect there'll be many a time when He, Himself, will take that little boy of yours into His lap, and let him know a love that makes all other loves seem puny by contrast. I wouldn't be at all surprised if the Heavenly Father keeps a few lollipops handy, for just such occasions!

And one day, you'll be greeted with a, "Hi, Mom! I've got some of the neatest things to show you! And some really fantastic people I can't wait for you to meet!"

Karen, I'm sure the next few weeks won't be easy—you can count on my prayers.

Love,
Mary Carol

19. MY FATHER'S WORLD

Scripture Reading: Psalm 24

"For lo, the winter is past, the rain is over and gone, the flowers appear on the earth, the time of the singing of birds is come and the voice of the turtle-dove is heard in our land" Song of Sol. 2:11, 12.

> Heaven above is softer blue, earth around is sweeter green!
> Something lives in every hue Christless eyes have never seen.
> Birds with gladder songs o'erflow, flowers with deeper beauties shine,
> Since I know as now I know, I am His, and He is mine.
>
> —Wade Robinson

Today, I noticed the tulips are coming up! The warm sun melts winter into puddles, and the devastating ice storm of a few weeks ago seems far away. We took a walk around the block, savoring spring with every step. Kristin spotted a robin. It has been one of those days for taking a deep breath, and saying, "Thanks, God, it's good to be alive."

I've wondered how being a "stranger and a pilgrim on this earth" fits in with the real pleasure of today. Here. Now. I've even had a twinge or two of guilt because I didn't *feel* more like a pilgrim. I've come to realize that, though polluted by sin so it is not all it might be, "this earth and all its fulness (the sunshine, the tulips, the robin) are the Lord's" (Ps. 24:1, Berk.). God has given us the good gifts of His creation to enjoy. C. S. Lewis, a long-time friend of mine through his books, has said, "Because we love something else more than this world, we love even this world better than those who know no other."

Get outside today! Find something of God's creation you can savor with your children.

20. IN MY FATHER'S HOUSE

Scripture Reading: John 14

"There are many rooms in my Father's House. If there were not, should I have told you that I am going away to prepare a place for you? It is true that I am going away to prepare a place for you, but it is just as true that I am coming again to welcome you into my own home" John 14:2, 3, Phillips.

"Mommy, do you know that Heaven is Jesus' House?" asked Kristin one day. "Yes," I replied. "And do you know, He has a little bed up there that's just my size? It's waiting for me. And He has a white blanket with orange flowers on it, just for me!"

The people that I know for whom Heaven is most real are either very young, like Kristin, or very old. (Interesting note: God's disclosure of what Heaven would be like was first given to the apostle John, who was probably in his nineties when he wrote the Book of Revelation.) From time to time, I've been able to catch a little Heavenly anticipation from some of these people. For myself, most of the time I get so bogged down with the daily routines of here and now that Heaven seems a little remote. A recent re-reading of C. S. Lewis's *The Last Battle* has helped me put the reality of Heaven into sharper focus. I highly recommend this book, along with the entire Narnia series, as reading for both you and your children. I quote a few selections here for a "taste-treat," to be read on a day when Heaven seems particularly distant to you.

"Listen, Peter. When Aslan said you could never go back to Narnia, he meant the Narnia you were thinking of. But that was not the real Narnia. That had a beginning and an end. It was only a shadow or a copy of the real Narnia, which has always been here: just as our own world, England and all, is only a shadow or copy of something in Aslan's real world. You need not mourn over Narnia, Lucy. All of the old Narnia that mattered, all the dear creatures, have been drawn into the real Narnia through the Door. And, of course, it is different; as different as a real thing is from a shadow or as waking life is from a dream.". . .

It was the Unicorn who summed up what everyone was feeling. He stamped his right fore-hoof on the ground and neighed and then cried: "I have come home at last! This is my real country! I belong here. This is the land I have been looking for all my life, though I never knew it till now. The reason why we loved the old Narnia is that it sometimes looked a little like this. Bree-hee-hee! Come further up, come further in!". . .

And there was greeting and kissing and old jokes revived (you've no idea how good an old joke sounds when you take it out again after a rest of five or six hundred years). . . .

And for us this is the end of all the stories, and we can most truly say that they all lived happily ever after. But for them it was only the beginning of the real story. All their life in this world, and all their adventures in Narnia had only been the cover and the title page: now at last they were beginning Chapter One of the Great Story, which no one on earth has read: which goes on for ever: in which every chapter is better than the one before.

—C. S. Lewis, *The Last Battle*
New York: Collier Books c. 1956

21. TO THE ELECT LADY...

Scripture Reading: II John

"This letter comes from the Elder to a certain Christian lady and her children, held in the highest affection not only by me but by all who know the truth"
II John 1:1, Phillips.

Some scholars and teachers feel that since the church is the bride of Christ, and the Greek word for church is feminine *(ecclēsia)*, John is writing here either to a local congregation, or to the church at large. For myself, I am reasonably certain that here we have one book that is specifically addressed to a Christian mother and her children.

> Some would have us believe that this lady and her children were really a church and its members; but verses 5, 10, and 12 convince us such an idea is far-fetched and artificial. We are glad that at least one little epistle in our New Testament is addressed to a Christian mother.
>
> —J. Sidlow Baxter*

Certainly the salutation in this epistle parallels the salutation in III John, which is clearly written to an individual, Gaius.

In any case, what is the message "to the elect lady and her children" (RSV)? John says: I'm not giving you new instructions; rather, I'm reminding you of something you already know. Love one another (v. 5).

At first glance, this might seem to be a bit superfluous. Of course mothers and children love each other! But, on second thought, maybe we need to be

*Baxter, J. Sidlow, *Explore the Book*
Grand Rapids: Zondervan 1960.

reminded anyway. A "veteran" mother once wisely said, "They won't remember whether the floor was always clean, but they will remember whether there was love in the house."

In another book, the apostle John states that others will know we are Christ's disciples if we have love one to another. Showing love must become our way of life! Sometimes I get so bogged down in the mechanics of running a household along with my extracurricular activities, that I forget what my real priorities are. Do my children know I love them, and does my love demonstrate to them that I belong to Christ?

John goes on to explain that we show our love by following God's commands. The mother he's writing to has evidently been teaching these commands to her children, for John says he rejoices that some of her children are walking in the truth.

John further says: Mother, beware who you entertain in your home. Be sure he is a follower of Christ's teaching. John is aware of how the people we associate with influence us and our children.

Mothers, families, writes John; the important thing for you to remember is to *love one another*.

22. WHY?

Scripture Reading: Isaiah 40

"My God, my God, why hast thou forsaken me?" Ps. 22:1.

"Why, Mommy?" Do you ever get tired of that question? I keep trying to tell myself that the only way my children will learn is by asking—and I do want them to have a healthy curiosity—but I must admit, I get tired of the "Whys" once in a while.

Like our own children, we as God's children often ask "Why?". Some of our "whys" are not without their humor; "Why am I so freckled, so tall, or so fat?" Others come from very heavy hearts. "Why was little Adam born with an open spine?" "Why did Ricky suffer so long with that brain tumor, and then die?" "Why did that automobile accident take Nancy's life?"

Since we are bound by time, and our vision and understanding are limited, some of the answers we receive from our Heavenly Father (who sees all of eternity in a glance) are difficult to understand. I don't pretend to understand any better than you do. I certainly don't have answers for some of these "Whys" that are spoken from troubled hearts. I would simply put before you one more "Why?"—this one asked by Isaiah, on behalf of God Himself.

"Why, Jacob, do you say, and why, Israel, do you declare, that your way is hidden from the Lord, that your rights are overlooked by your God? Do you not know, have you not heard? The Lord is the everlasting God, the Creator of the ends of the earth; He never faints or grows weary; His wisdom is unsearchable. He imparts vigor to the fainting, and to those who have no might He increases strength. Even youths shall faint and grow weary and young men go down exhausted; but they that await the Lord shall renew their strength. They shall mount up with wings like eagles; they shall run and not be weary; they shall walk and not faint" Isa. 40:27-31, Berk.

The Creator of the stars, the One who measured the waters in the hollow of His hand, is also the One who will gather the lambs in His arms, and carry them in His bosom.

A friend of mine with a sick daughter, could have bombarded God with "Whys." Instead, she said, "I keep telling myself, God loves Wendy far more perfectly than I ever could." Maybe that's the sort of thing we need to keep telling ourselves when our hearts are heavy with a "Why" that seems to have no answer.

Prayer: "This is my Father's world, O let me ne'er forget that though the wrong seems oft so strong, God is the ruler yet."

—Maltbie D. Babcock

23. STAINED GLASS, OR A MAGNIFYING GLASS?

Scripture Reading: Luke 1:26-56

"My soul doth magnify the Lord" Luke 1:46.

Scripture doesn't reveal a lot about Mary, the mother of Jesus. She was a descendant of David, engaged to Joseph, the carpenter, who was also of David's house. She was quite familiar with Hebrew scriptures, as she demonstrates in her song of praise (Luke 1:46-55) by freely quoting Hannah's song (I Sam. 2:1-8).

35

Mary must have known she would at the very least be criticized for conceiving a child before she was married—Mosaic law prescribed public accusation and death—yet she proclaimed, "My soul doth magnify the Lord, and my spirit is glad in God my Savior." When the angel came to tell her that the Holy Spirit would come upon her—that she would conceive a child who would therefore be the Son of God—her response was simply, "Here I am, the Lord's servant girl. Let it be with me as you say."

We know by their temple offering at the time of Jesus' birth (Luke 2:22-24) that Mary and Joseph were not wealthy. But young Mary must have been a reflective, thinking person; certainly, bearing the Son of God would give one occasion to reflect (Luke 2:19, 51).

We know that Mary turned to Jesus for help when the supply of wine for a wedding feast gave out (John 2:1-11). She pointed Jesus out to the servants, and told them to do whatever He commanded them.

We also know that Jesus' mother was faithful to Him at the time of His death; she stood by the cross as He died. Jesus spoke to her, and told the apostle John to carry out the eldest son's role of looking after her.

A stained glass window, although it does allow some light to pass through, calls attention to itself. A magnifying glass does not call attention to itself, but rather to the object being magnified. Mary's life falls into the second category. She was a mother who magnified the Lord.

24. JESUS, I'D LIKE YOU TO MEET JIMMY; JIMMY, THIS IS JESUS

Scripture Reading: Matthew 19:13-15

"Then little children were brought to Him so that He might lay His hands on them and pray" Matt. 13:13a, Berk.

Several of us were having coffee the other morning, and, as often happens, we began to talk about our children. But this time it wasn't about remedies for runny noses or the new fifth grade teacher. We wanted our children to meet Jesus. Sue expressed it for all of us when she said, "I know I can't force my faith on Jimmy. But I just want him to meet Jesus! I'd like Jesus to take his hand; and maybe put His hands on Jimmy's head."

So the next day we set off with our children to find Jesus. The children were excited at the prospect of a picnic. As we approached the place where Jesus was teaching, and saw the enormous crowds of people pressing in on Him, I began to have second thoughts. Even if we could get up close to Him, what chance was there that He would have time to speak personally to a handful of women and their children? But we persisted, and finally, somehow, we made our way through the crowd. I really felt foolish just before we reached the little knoll where Jesus was seated. Several of the disciples, acting as body guards, tried to push us away. One of them asked gruffly, "What do you think you're doing?" Close to tears, I blurted out, "We wanted our children to meet Jesus! I wanted Him to take Kristin's hand, and I was hoping He might hold Emily on His lap." "Can't you see He's busy?" responded the disciple, firmly, but a little more kindly. "He has so many important things to teach— He hasn't time to grant personal interviews, particularly to children."

We were about to leave when I saw Jesus looking in our direction, and realized He had heard our conversation. "Let the little children come to Me. Don't hold them back! The Kingdom of Heaven is made up of children such as these."

Jimmy, who is anything but shy, bounded forward, and was immediately by Jesus' side. Jesus asked Jimmy if he were taking good care of his mother while his father was away. I could tell that Jimmy really felt important. Jesus played "horse" with several of the children on his knee. Ruth, who had just finished nursing little Sarah, placed her in His arms. Kristin had brought her Raggedy Ann, and—I could hardly believe it—Jesus even had time to give Raggedy Ann a hug!

I don't think any of these children will have trouble putting their trust in Jesus. They know, first-hand, that He loves them, and that He thinks each of them is important.

Prayer: Heavenly Father, I wish I could lead my children to You in such a physical, tangible way. Please—since that isn't possible—help me to know the way to gently point them in Your direction. Thank you that You love little children!

25. THE HOUSE THAT THE LORD BUILDS

Scripture Reading: Psalm 127

"Unless the Lord builds the house, their labor is futile who build it" Ps. 127:1, Berk.

I don't want my labor to be futile—I want the Lord to be the builder of my house. But how would He go about building a house?

Before the foundation of the world, the Lord made a plan for the redemption of this house (I Peter 1:18-20).*

He intended this house to be built on the solid rock of His Word; that here His Word should be both heard, and put in practice (Matt. 7:24-25).

He would use building materials that have eternal value (Matt. 6:19-21).

He would have a man leave his father and mother, cling to his wife, and the two become one flesh (Gen. 2:24).

God would have this man love his wife as Christ loved the Church—which means putting his wife's welfare ahead of his own comforts and wishes; Christ was willing even to die for the sake of His Bride (Eph. 5:25, 28, 29).

God would have the wife put herself in *voluntary* submission to her husband; to put his interests and needs ahead of her own (Eph. 5:21-24).

God planned for children to be a part of this

*It is not my intent to play "Bible Hopscotch," and thereby distort the meaning of Scripture. I encourage you to examine carefully the Scripture passages used, in their context.

union, to extend and carry on the effect of the home even after the parents are gone (Ps. 127:3-5).

God wants the children of this house to obey and honor their parents (Eph. 6:1-3).

But God doesn't want the father to arouse his children's anger. He is not to "drive his children up the wall," as Francis Schaeffer puts it (Eph. 6:4).

God has given the father responsibility to see that his children are brought up in the instruction and admonition of the Lord (Eph. 6:4). This responsibility is not to be deferred to the wife!

This household is one that recognizes its dependence on the Lord (Ps. 127:1).

This is the house that the Lord builds.

Living Within Time:

26. GET YOUR PRIORITIES STRAIGHT

Scripture Reading: Luke 10:38-42

"But the Lord answered, 'Martha, Martha, you are fretting and fussing about so many things, but one thing is necessary. The part that Mary has chosen is best; and it shall not be taken away from her'" Luke 10:41, 42, NEB

I tend to be a "Martha." If Jesus and His disciples had needed a place to stay, I probably would have invited them to stay at our house (Luke 10:38). I probably would have fussed over the food, worried if I didn't have enough glasses to match, and been furious with my lazy sister!

Scripture records that Jesus rebuked Martha. He observed that she was anxious about many things, and said that Mary had chosen the better part. Did Jesus mean that Martha shouldn't have seen to the food at all? Should we, by implication, assume that taking care of people's physical needs is not important? I think not. I believe Jesus' criticism of Martha was, in part, directed at her attitude. Her activity could have been done to the glory of God, just as Mary's activity was. But Martha's attitude of anxiety and fretfulness could not bring glory to God. Jesus was also criticizing Martha's priorities. "Mary has chosen the better part." It would be better for you first to spend time with Me, Jesus was saying.

Have you ever had a lot of company, and ended up so involved with the details—sheets, towels, dishes, food—that you didn't really have time to spend with the people? I have done that. Jesus is saying to all of us Marthas: That is a mistake; get your priorities straight. Spend time with me. Make time for people. I will then give you enough time to take care of those things which are really necessary.

Martin Luther said that when he had a particularly busy day, he got up even earlier to spend time with God. I have found that if I take the time to meet God, and get in a right relationship with Him *first,* my relationships with people and things fall into place much more smoothly.

I have also found that when I am overwhelmed with things to do, it helps to make a mental list of tasks, and rank them according to their importance. That way, I don't waste a lot of time on a low priority activity.

Jesus was trying to teach Martha that people take

priority over things. Things are only important because they help us minister to people. It is important, therefore, that I do the laundry today, so my family can have warm, dry clothing to wear tomorrow. But it is more important for me to spend time listening to my teenager when he wants to talk than for me to get the floor waxed.

Jesus said, "Seek ye first the kingdom of God and His righteousness, and all these things shall be added unto you." Time is part of "all these things." Jesus will grant us Marthas the time to attend to the necessary details, if we seek Him first.

Living Within Time:

27. DON'T GET WORN OUT

Scripture Reading: Ecclesiastes 3

"What benefit does the workman get from that for which he wears himself out?" Eccles. 3:9, Berk.

This is a beautiful little verse, tucked away in Ecclesiastes 3, the "time chapter." The same thought is expressed in a little different way by the writer of Psalm 127. "It is useless for you to be early in rising while being late in sitting up, eating the bread of toil; for He gives His loved ones sleep" (Ps. 127:2, Berk.). God doesn't intend for us to be worn out! Sleep is a gift of God. The tasks God intends for us to do can be done without our always being tired. If we are in a perpetual state of weariness, something is wrong, and we need to re-examine our lives.

Get enough sleep tonight! God will take care of tomorrow. You need not be awake to see that the new day arrives.

If your weariness is more than just physical, think about the implications this promise has for you:

> "But they that wait upon the Lord shall renew their strength; they shall mount up with wings as eagles; they shall run, and not be weary; and they shall walk, and not faint!" Isa. 40:31.

Living Within Time:

28. IS YOUR HOUSE IN ORDER?

Scripture Reading: Ecclesiastes 3

"For God is not a God of confusion . . ." I Cor. 14:33, RSV.

"Let all things be done decently and in order" I Cor. 14:40.

Our God is a God of order. The order and balance in the universe He created is one demonstration of this. When man sinned, this God of order introduced a plan for redeeming mankind. The remainder of Scripture unfolds the details and fulfillment of that plan.

It would seem reasonable, then, that if God doesn't operate in a haphazard fashion, neither should we. Much as I begrudge the time spent cleaning out or organizing closets and drawers, I have found that in the long run I end up saving time.

Just as God "planned ahead" for the redemption of mankind, we should learn to plan ahead. Planning a week's meals in advance, then making a list and shopping for those items needed; preparing food ahead of time, and freezing it; knowing that the baby will be fussy just prior to supper, so getting supper preparation started earlier in the day—these are a few examples of doing things decently and in order. Planning ahead does eliminate a lot of inefficiency and wasted time.

God's Word tells us to do things "in order." This kind of planning and putting our house in order can be—and should be—done as an offering to God.

Recommended Reading: How to Find the Time, by Pat King: Aglow Publications. I have found this book, written by a mother of ten children, to be very helpful.

Living Within Time:

29. A DAY AT A TIME

Scripture Reading: Proverbs 31

"As thy days, so shall thy strength be" Deut. 33:25b.

"...there is a proper time for every project under heaven" Eccles. 3:1b, Berk.

As I read Proverbs 31, I became more and more frustrated. The number of things this "ideal woman" accomplished seemed incredible. It would be impossible for me to come anywhere *close* to doing all this mother did. Did God just put this chapter here to tease us?

A study of the background of this chapter proved helpful.* What may be obvious to some readers finally occurred to me: this chapter represents a lifetime! The Proverbs 31 mother surely didn't accomplish all of those things in a single day, or even in a single year! The writer of Ecclesiastes assures us that there is a time for everything. In Deuteronomy we are promised, "As thy days, so shall thy strength be." God doesn't expect me to tackle more than one day at a time. He will give me enough time.

When faced with a particularly heavy week, I have found it helpful to list, either mentally or on paper, all the things that absolutely have to be done, and then the extra things I'd like to get done if possible. I then divide my list into the seven days, usually with a plan for both morning and afternoon. Tackling only one day (or sometimes a half day) at a time cuts the pressure of a demanding week or month down considerably.

"Do not fret, therefore, in view of tomorrow, for tomorrow will have its own anxieties. The day's peculiar troubles suffice for that day" (Matt. 6:34, Berk.).

*In understanding Proverbs 31, it is important to note that this passage is an acrostic poem, or alphabetic ode. Each line begins with a different Hebrew letter in consecutive order. This naturally limits what can be said about the woman; such structure is more restrictive than straight prose.

The writer of this passage, according to verse 1, is King Lemuel. No one is certain who Lemuel was, although the traditional view is that King Lemuel was King Solomon. In any case, the writer was probably not describing his own wife, since some of the activities attributed to this woman were not exactly queenly duties.

Living Within Time:

30. GOD ISN'T BOUND BY MY TIME TABLE

Scripture Reading: Psalm 37:1-8

"My times are in Thy hand" Psalm 31:15a.

On the day a friend of mine was to be released from the hospital, he discovered that his doctor had forgotten to sign the release papers, and could not be reached. My friend had to remain in his hospital bed. Important things were being left undone! A day was being wasted! It would have been easy to fuss and fume. But that day my friend received a new roommate, a man who was desperately needy, and ready to confront the claims of Jesus Christ. As a result of this "wasted day," the roommate put his trust in Christ.

Despite our well-laid plans, God sometimes intervenes. What we think is the right time may not turn out to be God's time. Lists are helpful, but we must recognize that Christ, not the list, is our Lord and Master. We need to wait on Him, trusting our time-table to the hands of the One who sees all of Eternity in a glance. Then we need to relax!

"Commit your way unto the Lord; trust in Him, too, and He will bring it about" Ps. 37:5, Berk.

46

31. A CASE FOR BREAKFAST

Scripture Reading: Proverbs 31

"She gets up before dawn to prepare breakfast for her household" Proverbs 31:15, LB.

I must admit, I'm *not* the sort of person who bounces out of bed every morning, cheerful, efficient, and ready to go! More often than not, it is a real effort to drag myself up, and I go through a period of not being altogether awake. But I do believe in breakfast, both nutritionally and psychologically!

I'm no nutrition expert, but I've been told that one should "eat like a king at breakfast, and like a pauper at dinner." Most Americans do it in reverse, I think.

Breakfast is a new beginning. As a family or as individual members, we may have "blown it" yesterday, but this is a new day, a fresh start. Yesterday's problems may not all be solved today, but today we have a chance to look at them with a fresh perspective. Some days breakfast is the only time I see my husband—so I've always made it a point to get up to fix him breakfast, regardless of how early, even if it means I have to serve a second shift to the rest of the family. I'm not very talkative in the early morning, but I think breakfast together, even if mostly silent, can be a supportive "I'm rooting for you today" sort of statement.

I am amazed at the amount of energy demonstrated by the Proverbs 31 woman. Verse 17 (NEB) says, "She sets about her duties with vigor, and braces herself for the work." I can testify that a good breakfast is a pretty good "bracer," and that I am usually most productive after breakfast!

Have a good breakfast today!

32. A MOTHER WITH OUTSIDE EMPLOYMENT

Scripture Reading: Proverbs 31

"She considers a field and buys it; with the fruit of her hands she plants a vineyard. . . . She sees that her merchandise is profitable. . . . She makes linen garments and sells them . . . Proverbs 31:16, 18, 24, Berk.

I don't wish to get involved in a debate over the pros and cons of mothers with outside employment. I myself stopped teaching school about a month before Kristin was born, and have not been salaried since then. However, I still bristle when people say, "You're not working any more?" because I think a good case could be made for the fact that I probably work harder now! But to those who maintain that "a woman's place is only in the home," it is interesting to take a look at the "Ideal Woman" described in Proverbs 31. She is a mother, (v. 11) and her children evidently feel she is a good mother. "Her children rise up and call her blessed" (v. 28, Berk.).

Look at this mother's "outside employment." V. 16: "After careful thought, she buys a field and plants a vineyard out of her earnings" (NEB). V. 18: "She sees that her business goes well" (NEB). V. 24: "She

48

weaves linen, and sells it, and supplies merchants with their sashes" (NEB). The writer of Proverbs concludes, "Extol her for the fruit of all her toil, and let her labours bring her honour in the city gate."

It is not clear at what point in the lives of her children this mother carried on these activities, but it is clear that she had outside interests. She was a good businesswoman, and for this she must have had to spend time away from her home. The rest of the chapter makes it clear that her family has not been neglected; it is, in fact, thriving.

I know some mothers who feel guilty because they have found it necessary to supplement the family income with outside work. I want to say to them, "Be sure that before God your priorities are in order; and then if they are, *don't feel guilty!* Keep your eyes and ears open. You can enrich your children with what you see and learn, as well as with what you earn." I've long been a believer that the quality of time spent with my children is far more important than the quantity.

What about those of us who don't bring home a paycheck? I think there is a real lesson for us here in Proverbs—we need to have interests outside our homes and families. To be able to give wise advice (v. 26) our horizons need to be a little wider than our own four walls. I have found I can go at my "mothering" with greater gusto after I've had a little break from it!

Today, or someday soon, leave your children with a baby sitter, and do something to broaden your own horizons!

33. EVE ... MOTHER OF EVERY LIVING PERSON

Scripture Reading: Genesis 2:21-23; 3:15-24; 4:1, 2

"The man named his wife Eve [life] because she became the mother of every living person" Gen. 3:20, Berk.

Can you imagine if there was *no one* to assure you, "First babies are usually late" or "Don't worry, the morning sickness only lasts the first couple months" or "You're carrying the baby low—that means it's probably a boy," or to discuss the pros and cons of natural childbirth, or a certain obstetrician, or one type of diaper over another? This was the situation in which Eve found herself!

Eve was the only woman ever to know what it was like to live in an unfallen state. So her suffering as she realized the consequences of sin must have been profound.

It is interesting to note that Eve did not receive a name until after God had spelled out the results of Adam's and her sin. I think the fact that Eve means "life" is significant, especially in light of the fact that her sin and Adam's brought death into the world. Eve's suffering for sin was unique, but God in His mercy gave her a very special promise, a very special hope. God told the group assembled in the garden that He would put enmity between the serpent and the woman; that from the seed of the woman would come One who would crush the serpent (Satan), and who would be the ultimate victor over sin, despite the attempt of the serpent to lash out at Him (bruise His heel—Gen. 3:15).

God, through a child of mother Eve, introduced the world once again to the hope of Life. Eve's hope can be ours as we appropriate the Eternal Life earned by Jesus Christ, son of God and son of Eve!

> "For the wages of sin is death; but the gift of God in Christ Jesus our Lord is eternal life"
>
> Rom. 6:23, Berk.

> "And this is eternal life: To know Thee, the only true God and Jesus Christ whom Thou hast sent"
>
> John 17:3, Berk.

34. WANT SOME CHERRIES, GOD!

Scripture Reading: I Thessalonians 5:16-18;
Ephesians 3:14-21

"Under all circumstances give thanks, for such is God's will for you in Christ Jesus" I Thess. 5:18, Berk.

Emily had been awfully quiet for about a half hour. When I went to investigate, I discovered her on the back porch, with the quart of cherries we had just purchased at the market. She had eaten half of the cherries. I took the remaining cherries from her, explaining, "Emily, you have had enough cherries for today. If you eat any more, you will get sick." But all Emily could understand was that she had been deprived of something which from her perspective was good, sweet, and desirable. "Want some cherries, Mom. Please! More cherries!" Even the "magic word" fell on what must have seemed to her like deaf ears. Then the tears came, and she began to pound the floor in anger and frustration. . . .

51

I can remember asking God for "cherries." Things I was certain were good and desirable. And I can remember thinking my prayers fell on deaf ears. Like Emily, I became angry and frustrated, unable to accept God's "Not now" as an answer. In years to come, Emily will understand why I didn't want her to eat a quart of cherries at one sitting! Sometimes God allows us to see, in retrospect, why He answered our prayers as He did. Other hard-to-understand answers will have to wait until we reach heaven!

Have you been asking God for "cherries"? Can you accept His answer? Can you give thanks for what God has seemingly denied, confident that He will utilize His abundant power to work out what is best for you?

Prayer: "Now unto him who by the power at work within us is able to do far more abundantly than all we ask or think, to him be glory in the Church and in Christ Jesus to all generations for ever and ever. Amen" Eph. 3:20, 21, RSV.

35. WHATEVER HAPPENED TO THE MOTHER OF HOPHNI AND PHINEHAS?

Scripture Reading: I Samuel 2:12-36; 4:17

"However, the sons of Eli were the sons of Belial [worthlessness]; they showed no regard for the Lord" I Sam. 2:12, Berk.

I'm a "Missionary Kid," so I guess I'm entitled to make the observation that all too often, the children of missionaries and ministers grow up "showing no regard for the Lord." Why is that?

Hophni and Phinehas were "priest's kids"—and their behavior, as described in I Samuel 2, was despicable. We don't know much about what kind of a father Eli was, and we know nothing about the boys' mother. Whether Eli really condoned their conduct, or whether the boys were pulling the wool over his eyes is unclear. When Eli did give them a mild scolding— the people were beginning to talk—it fell on deaf ears. All we can really do is speculate—but I wonder if Eli wasn't like too many of his modern counterparts, so busy doing "the Lord's Work" that they forget that their families, too, are "the Lord's Work."

I walked in one day as three-year-old Kristin was playing with her dolls. I asked her what she was doing. She replied, "I'm having a Worship Committee meeting." (For two years, John and I have been actively involved in the Worship Committee of our church.) We've laughed over this incident, but it has given us pause to reflect: are we too active in too many "church activities"? Are our children suffering because of it?

Today, think about your priorities and activities. Are your children getting shortchanged?

36. ON BEING LIBERATED

Scripture Reading: John 8:25-36

"If you adhere to my teaching, you will truly be my disciples; you will know the truth, and the truth will

set you free ... If the Son liberates you, then you are unquestionably free" John 8:31, 32, 36, Berk.

We have about fifteen tropical fish living within the confines of a twenty-gallon aquarium. Suppose one day I said, "Fish, I feel sorry for you cooped up in that tank. I want you to be free. Have the run of the house; even go outdoors if you like!" Those fish were created for a certain environment. For them, freedom can be found only within that environment. To go outside it is certain death.

Like the fish, human beings have been created to find freedom only within a certain context. That context is a right relationship with God.

Much has been spoken and written in the last few years about "Women's Liberation." I believe that the Christian is the only person who can really understand what liberation is all about. When I taught school, I knew some women who felt "tied to their jobs"—anything but liberated. Now that I have joined the ranks of unsalaried wives and mothers, I'm finding that situation too, leaves some women feeling stifled and tied down. So I have come to the conclusion that being liberated has very little to do with one's actual occupation. The Christian (man or woman) who believes he or she was created by God, has found reconciliation with God, and is living to glorify God, is the only person who can be truly liberated. Any other kind of liberation is at best a temporary thing, and can lead to an end as absurd as that of the fish, liberated to have the run of the house.

Today, take hold of this truth: "If the Son liberates you, then you are unquestionably free."

37. BUT I DON'T FEEL LIBERATED!

Scripture Reading: John 8:25-36

"If the Son liberates you, then you are unquestionably free" John 8:36, Berk.

I still believe all those things I wrote yesterday. But I don't feel very liberated. I was sick in the night—but mothers of small children can't indulge in the luxury of staying in bed for a day. So I dragged myself out of bed, made breakfast, and dressed the kids anyway. I have piles of dirty laundry undone, and stacks of dishes in the sink. Emily has a cold, and is getting a tooth, so her disposition doesn't help mine. John has been so busy this past week he hasn't had time to show much compassion, or to appreciate half of what I do. All he seems to notice is the button that didn't get sewed on, or the pants that didn't get pressed. I don't have money enough to pay the overdue gas bill. HELP! What can I grab onto that will help me today?

First—I am not in this alone; God is with me. The writer of Hebrews (talking about money problems, but it certainly can be applied to any sort of difficulty) says, "He has said, 'I will never give you up, or ever at all desert you,' so that we are to say boldly, 'The Lord is my Helper, I will not fear! What can man do to me?" (Heb. 13:5b, 6, Berk.). James 1:5 tells us that if we lack wisdom, we are to ask of God, and He will grant it. I can go to God with my frustrations, confident that He is big enough for them. He has been tested in all points like as we are, and He knows how to empathize. I can ask Him to help me with my attitude.

Second—I am not in this alone, I'm a member of the Body of Christ. The left wrist can do double duty if the right wrist is broken. "When one member suffers, all the members share the suffering. When a member is honored, they all share the joy.... You are Christ's body, and members with assigned parts" I Cor. 12:26-27, Berk. Maybe there's a friend I can call who could pray for me. Maybe there's a friend I could call who would drop by and give me some help.

Third—I am *positionally* free, even when I don't feel it. I am God's child, and I believe He has put me in this place. If the Creator of all the universe has assigned me to wash Emily's diapers, and if my fulfillment of that assignment somehow pleases Him and brings Him glory, then that is no mean task. "If the Son liberates you, then you are unquestionably free."

You know, I feel a little better already!

38. "LOVE . . . IS NOT POSSESSIVE"

Scripture Reading: I Samuel 1:19-28

"I have therefore handed him back to the Lord; as long as he lives he is returned to the Lord" I Sam. 1:28, Berk.

One morning, armed with rags, rubber gloves,

scouring pad, and oven cleaner, I knelt in front of my dirty oven. Somehow it just didn't "wipe clean" like the commercials say. Kristin came along just then, gave me a big hug, and said, "I love you, Mommy." We spent a few moments enjoying each other's company, and somehow, even the oven didn't seem so bad after that! The love of a very young child is one of the special rewards of being a mother.

Yet that love, beautiful as it is, was not meant for us to hoard and clutch to ourselves. Love has a unique property—giving it away doesn't diminish the supply! Our children are a gift from God, and, while we would never want to reject their love, we have a responsibility to direct some of their love to God.

Hannah is a good example of a mother who recognized this responsibility. She was even willing for Samuel, her long awaited and only son, to be brought up in the temple. It was Hannah's desire that as Samuel grew up, worship of God would be a large part of his daily routine.

We can't "return our children to the Lord" in exactly the way Hannah did, but we can direct their thoughts and their love to Him by making God part of their everyday lives. "God loves you! He made the wheat to grow so we could have flour to make your birthday cake." "God must have laughed when He made those funny monkeys." "Jesus is sad when He sees you grabbing Emily's doll away from her."

Today, think of something specific you could do or say to direct your child's love to God.

39. NOT PHONY

Scripture Reading: II Timothy 1:1-5; 3:14-17;
Acts 16:1-5

*"I thank God ... when I call to remembrance the un-
feigned faith that is in thee, which dwelt first in thy
grandmother Lois, and thy mother Eunice; and I am
persuaded that in thee also"* II Tim. 1:5.

Eunice was a mother in a difficult position. She was
a Jewish believer with an unbelieving Greek husband.
So the responsibility of leading her son Timothy to
trust in God fell solely upon her shoulders.

Paul makes mention of her strong faith (II Tim.
1:5) and is confident of the quality of Timothy's early
teaching (II Tim. 3:14). "Remember from what sort
of people your knowledge has come, and how from
early childhood your mind has been familiar with the
holy scriptures, which can open the mind to the sal-
vation which comes through belief in Christ Jesus"
(II Tim. 3:14, 15, Phillips). It is significant that Eunice herself probably did not have access to written
copies of Scripture. I look at the five or six different
translations of Scripture, the concordances and com-
mentaries to which I have access—and I'm not sure
I'm doing as good a job as Eunice did! She must have
committed many portions to memory, otherwise she
would have had difficulty teaching Timothy. Yet rote
memory, and head knowledge, as important as they
are, don't produce a changed life.

What was Eunice's secret? The King James version
describes her faith, and that of Timothy as "unfeigned." Not phony. I'd like to think she was the
kind of mother who, if she lost her temper could

say, "I'm sorry, Timothy, what I said wasn't Christ-like." When times of discouragement hit—perhaps as she struggled with ways to share her faith with her husband—I'd like to think Eunice could say, "I'm really low today, Timothy. I know God's promises are true, but I sure don't feel it today. Pray with me!" Eunice would not have been one to utter empty spiritual platitudes—had she done this, her faith would not have attracted Timothy—for children are quick to spot, and shun, "phonies."

It's possible my children might learn something about baking cookies from my verbal explanation. They will certainly learn more by watching me actually make the cookies. But they will learn the most as we stand, side by side, and make cookies together. The same principle applies to any kind of learning.

Eunice certainly must have made sure Timothy heard the Scripture read and preached. And she must have demonstrated her "unfeigned" faith before Timothy's watching eyes. Then, together, they walked side by side, living out their faith and applying it to each day's joys and problems in such a way that Paul commends them for a faith that is real—not phony.

40. WHAT'LL I DO IF?

Scripture Reading: I Kings 17:7-16

"As thy days, so shall thy strength be" Deut. 33:25.

I struggle at times with the "What'll I do if" type of worry. I remember two such occasions while I was pregnant with Kristin. Once, I worried when I saw a child who had been born without legs—and again when a friend gave birth to a child who was mentally retarded. I worried about what I would do if my child were born handicapped. I was afraid I couldn't cope with the situation. This past December, my children were exposed to chicken pox, and were due to have it the week of Christmas—which was the time when my entire family, for the first Christmas in ten years, was planning to visit us. I did battle with "What'll I do if" quite a few times, especially when my pediatrician assured me that chicken pox was highly contagious, and the children were almost certain to get it!

The unnamed mother mentioned in I Kings 17, known to us only as a widow of Zarephath, certainly had cause to ask herself, "What'll I do if?". There was famine in the land, and she had no source for more food. She was preparing to bake her last loaf of bread for herself and her son, and she then fully expected to die. Along came a stranger who asked her to give him her last loaf; if she would do so, God would see to it that her flour and oil supply would not give out. Now I have no problem giving a meal to a stranger, but my last loaf of bread? Surely my child should come before some stranger! And if a stranger would say to me what Elijah did to this woman, I'm enough of a skeptic that I suspect my response would be, "You've got to be kidding!" I probably would have missed out on the miracle altogether.

I think it is significant that Scripture does not say that the flour barrel and the oil jug would always be *full*. All that was promised was that she would have *enough* when she needed it, not a surplus beforehand. I am certain I do not now have the strength and wisdom to cope with a handicapped child. But I am also equally certain, that should God choose to give me such a child, on that day He would also grant ample strength and wisdom to meet such a challenge.

If you, too, do battle with "What'll I do if," write out Deuteronomy 33:25 and place it above your sink, or in some other prominent place.

41. BEND DOWN AND LISTEN

Scripture Reading: Psalm 17

"I have called on Thee, O God, for Thou wilt answer me. Incline Thine ear to me; hear my words" Ps. 17:6.

"He that keepeth Israel will neither slumber, nor sleep" Ps. 121:4.

"Mommy, listen to me! Quit saying Uh huh, and give me an answer!" How many of us Mommies are guilty of tuning out our children's chatter, punctuating it only with a few well-spaced uh huhs? I'm certainly glad God doesn't treat us that way. Have you ever noticed how frequently the phrase, "Incline Thine ear to me" occurs in the Psalms? Bend down and listen to me! And our Heavenly Father bends His ear, listens, and answers. What an example for us as parents!

Good listening often takes some bending—getting down to the same level. I've found that squatting, or sitting down on the floor with my young children

61

aids greatly in our communication. The psalmist here is confident not only that God will bend His ear, but that He will listen, and answer. Real listening is work! It requires concentration. It takes time. It is one way to say, "I love you."

42. DISCOVER GREEN

"To every living creature that creeps on the earth I have given the green vegetation for food" Gen. 1:30b, Berk.

"He maketh me to lie down in green pastures" Ps. 23:2.

"I [God] look after him with watchful care; I am like an evergreen cypress; and your fruit, it is found, comes from me" Hos. 14:8b, Berk.

"Mommy! Mommy! I found Green!" shouted Kristin delightedly. Responding to the excitement, I soon learned that Kristin, on her own, had discovered that blue crayon mixed with yellow crayon would produce green. I'm certain she was as excited as the very first person who ever mixed the two pigments together, and her excitement was infectious. Together we began to look for all the greens we could find—noting that some were more yellow, others more blue. Our search led us outdoors, where the first green leaves were beginning to appear on trees, and green grass had finally replaced the winter's blanket of snow.

> Green is an olive
> And a pickle

The sound of green
Is a water-trickle
Green is the world
After the rain
Bathed and beautiful
Again . . .
Under a grape arbor
Air is green
With sprinkles of sunlight
In between.
Green is the meadow,
Green is the fuzz
That covers up
Where winter was. . .
—Mary O'Neill*

I'm glad God made green—and blue, and red, and gold, and purple. Just think what the world would be like if it were all black, white, and various shades of gray! Green is one of God's good gifts.

"Every good gift and every perfect gift is from above, and cometh down from the Father of lights"
James 1:17.

Prayer: Thank You, God, for the eyes to see, and the ability to discover. Thank You for Your gift of Green.

*O'Neill, Mary, "What is Green?" *Hailstones and Halibut Bones,* New York: Doubleday, c. 1961.

43. COME CLOSER!

Scripture Reading: Matthew 11:28-30

"Draw near to God, and He will draw near you"
James 4:8, Berk.

I wonder how many generations of little girls have complained, "Ow, Mom, you're pulling my hair!" as the pig-tails, or curls were being combed into place. And how many mothers have replied, "Come closer to me instead of backing off, and it won't hurt so much."

How like our Heavenly Father! Sometimes it seems that He has an awful lot of snarls to comb out of our lives. Snarls of pride, self-pity, gossip. Yet He says, Come closer, child, and it won't hurt so much. Try being yoked closely to me. You'll be surprised how easy it is; for taking My yoke means you have Me with you, to help bear the hurts.

I was trying to cope with a snarl of self-pity the other day. I thought I could work through it, myself. The last thing I wanted to do was to read my Bible, or pray. And the snarl became all the snarlier until I realized what a mistake I was making.

> "Come to Me all you who labor and are heavily burdened, and I will rest you. Take my yoke on you, and learn from Me, for I am gentle and humble of heart, and you will find rest for your souls, for my yoke is easy, and my burden is light"
>
> Matt. 11:28-30, Berk.

As you fold the laundry, or clean the refrigerator today, think what wearing Christ's yoke means to you, personally.

44. ETERNAL FOOTPRINTS

Scripture Reading: Matthew 6:19-24

"But lay up for yourselves treasures in heaven where

no moth or rust destroy, and where thieves do not dig through and steal" Matt. 6:20, Berk.

After breakfast, I wiped off the high chair, and washed the floor under it. After our cookie-making venture, I wiped off the high chair, and washed the floor under it. After lunch, I wiped off the high chair, and washed the floor under it. We've just finished supper, and to look at the high chair, and the floor under it, you'd never know how many times today I wiped off that tray, and washed that floor!

In most other jobs, a person can look back at the end of a day, and see what he or she has accomplished. A secretary can count the letters she's typed; a teacher can reflect on the lessons she's prepared; a factory worker can count the finished products at the end of the assembly line. And nearly everyone (except mothers) can count up the paycheck at the end of the week. I think that for me, one of the most frustrating things about being a mother is the jobs that I have to do over and over, without anything to show for them.

In high school I first encountered Longfellow's "Psalm of Life," in which the poet expresses at least a desire for, if not a belief in, eternal life and achievements that last. The end of the poem reads:

> "Lives of great men all remind us we can
>   make our lives sublime
> And, departing, leave behind us foot-
>   prints on the sands of time."

I wonder if Longfellow had ever been near the beach —I've never observed any footprints in sand that didn't soon get washed away. Perhaps he really felt that all anyone could do was to make a footprint that, at best, lasts for a short time.

We who believe in eternity (John 3:15-18; 36), and who have children, are one up on Longfellow. For our children will live eternally. Wiping off the high chair, and washing the floor under it is, undeniably, one of the dull and frustrating aspects of motherhood. But let's get things in perspective. A far more important aspect of motherhood is the chance—for a brief time—to influence a life that will last eternally. Most of the letters typed, lesson plans prepared, products off an assembly line and paychecks are of the footprints in the sand variety. A child is an eternal footprint. Let that thought grab you the next time you're wiping up after your child!

45. MOVING DAY

Scripture Reading: Hebrews 1:10-12

"Jesus Christ is the same, yesterday and today and forever" Heb. 13:8, RSV.

In this age of increasing mobility, many families move from place to place several times during the growing up years of the children. Moving can be an unsettling thing. New place, new friends, new schools, new job, new house. At least today, unlike Abram, we are able to learn a great deal about the place to which we are going before we leave. Usually the guidance we receive from God isn't as verbally explicit for us as it was for Abram, and we can involve the whole family in prayer for God's direction as a move is contemplated.

At these times when everything seems in transition, nothing is like it used to be, schedules are disrupted, and painful goodbyes have to be said; we who are Christians have something familiar to cling to. "Jesus Christ is the same, yesterday and today and forever." Surely Jesus Christ knows what it is to leave home and all that is familiar, and can empathize with us.

If you are moving, I offer as a "going away present" a hymn which has been a favorite one of mine as I have ended and begun new chapters in my life:

Be still, my soul: the Lord is on thy side;
Bear patiently the cross of grief or pain;
Leave to Thy God to order and provide,
In every change He faithful will remain.
Be still my soul; thy best, thy heavenly Friend,
Through thorny ways leads to a joyful end.

Be still, my soul: thy God doth undertake
To guide the future, as He has the past.
Thy hope, thy confidence let nothing shake;
All now mysterious shall be bright at last.
Be still my soul: the waves and winds still know
His voice who ruled them while He dwelt below.

Be still my soul: the hour is hast'ning on
When we shall be forever with the Lord;
When disappointment, grief and fear are gone,
Sorrow forgot, love's purest joys restored.
Be still, my soul: when change and tears are past,
All safe and blessed we shall meet at last.

—Katharina von Schlegel
Tr. by Jane L. Borthwick

46. I'M SORRY...

Scripture Reading: Matthew 5:23; Ephesians 6:4

"If thou bring thy gift to the altar, and there remem-berest that thy brother hath aught against thee; leave there thy gift before the altar, and go thy way; first be reconciled with thy brother, and then come and offer thy gift" Matt. 5:23.

Company was coming and I was busy vacuuming, picking up toys, and whisking them out of sight. But Kristin had something to say to me. She walked away with tears in her eyes after finding she couldn't be heard over the roar of the vacuum. After struggling with the thought that I couldn't possibly be ready by 6 o'clock—and feeling like a terrible mother—I shut off the vacuum and went in to tell Kristin I was sorry for not listening earlier, and I heard what she had to say.

It's always hard to say "I'm sorry," and saying it to one's own child is no exception. I disagree with the thought expressed in the popular song, "Love means you'll never have to say you're sorry." While real love demands that I don't bear grudges even if someone doesn't say he's sorry to me (Eph. 4:32), saying "I'm sorry" may sometimes be necessary to heal and continue to build a real love relationship (Matt. 5:23).

D. L. Moody knew what it was to say, "I'm sorry." The story is told of how anxious he was to have a grassy lawn at his home in Northfield, Massachusetts —a lawn like those he had admired in England. One day his sons accidentally let their horses loose from the barn. The horses galloped all over the grass, and destroyed it. Father Moody lost his temper with the boys. But after they had gone to bed that night, he came up to their room and said, "I want you to forgive me; that wasn't the way Christ taught."

Are you ready, able, and willing to say, "I'm sorry" to your child today, should the occasion demand it?

47. EXPECTANT PRAYER

Scripture Reading: Acts 12:1-17

"I will do whatever you may ask in My name" John 14:14, Berk.

In the days of the early church, it was quite a different thing than it is today for a mother to open her home for a prayer meeting. She, and those gathered there, did so at the risk of their lives. Yet that is what Mary, the mother of John Mark, did when the apostle Peter was put in prison.

This passage has always given me a chuckle—but it is usually a short-lived chuckle when I realize how many of my prayers are just as limited in their expectations. Maybe that's why God tells us to come as little children. Young children are so vulnerable, and so trusting. And we, their parents, know that God doesn't always answer prayers with a "yes." So, we try, in our wisdom, to shield them from possible disappointment. One mother said she was afraid to suggest her daughter pray for God's help in finding a lost article, because she, herself, had already searched the house, and was certain it couldn't be found. Then there was Sarah, a young friend of Kristin's who had lost her cat. The cat had been missing for a number of days, and Sarah's mother feared the cat was gone for good; but Sarah wanted to pray—and did—that God would send her cat back. The cat returned that day, unharmed! We could all learn from the little Sarahs God has given us.

"The earnest prayer of a righteous person has great effect" James 5:16b, Berk.

48. GUARDIAN ANGELS

Scripture Reading: Psalm 91

"For He gives His angels orders regarding you, to protect you wherever you go. They will support you with their hands lest you strike your foot against a stone" Ps. 91:11, 12, Berk.

I believe in guardian angels! After a long, weary day, I finally managed to rock Emily, who was sick with a high fever, to sleep. As I laid her carefully in bed, I said, inside myself, "O.K. angels, you'll have to take over from here. I don't have any energy left." Emily and I both had a good night's sleep.

Yesterday, someone inadvertently left the back door open. My adventurous Emily was out, and in no time found her way to the street, where she was discovered a short time later, unharmed. (Emily keeps her angel pretty busy!)

I don't remember ever discussing angels with my parents; but I'm sure they must have believed in them. There were many nights when their yearbook editor daughter worked late at school; then traveled across Tokyo on busses and trains, long after dark. I remember them praying for safe keeping, but I don't ever remember them showing real anxiety.

One word of caution: God will not necessarily do a miracle just because we have done something foolish, or rash. He often allows us to suffer the natural consequences of our actions. God expects us to use the common sense He's given us. Satan, in Matthew 4:5-7, tempts Jesus to jump off the top of the temple. He tells Jesus that God's angels will support Him, and quotes Psalm 91:11, 12. Jesus responds by telling Satan not to tempt God. For us to try to tempt God would be equally wrong.

When the responsibilities of being a mother start to overwhelm me, I am grateful that He, who watches over His children, "Slumbers not, nor sleeps." I am also very thankful that He has put His angels in charge of watching over us, and our children.

49. YOU ARE LIGHT

Scripture Reading: Matthew 5:14-16; John 9:5b

"Let your light so shine before men, that they may see your good works and give glory to your Father who is in Heaven" Matt. 5:16, RSV.

When I graduated from high school, I envisioned myself as, at the very least, a several-thousand-watt beacon light, such as those used along airport runways. By the time I had completed my first year of teaching elementary school, I concluded that I was only a small flashlight, and a flickering one at that. I was ready to head for the nearest bushel basket!

"Let your light so shine," we are commanded. But sometimes I feel so alone, so inadequate. God has to remind me, like He did Elijah (I Kings 19:1-18), that when He says "You are the light of the world," it is a plural "you," not a singular. During the first manned space flights which orbited the earth, I remember how entire cities turned on all their lights as a beacon to the men in the space capsule. What one single light could not have accomplished, many lights, in concert, could accomplish.

"Let your light so shine," we are commanded. But I'm just a small, flickering flashlight. God could surely do without me, couldn't He? I'm afraid of offending people; I'm afraid of coming on too strong. Jesus Himself said, "Men love darkness rather than light because their deeds are evil." It would be a lot more comfortable under that bushel basket! "Let your light so shine," was what He said; not, "Everybody except Mary Loeks, let your light shine." The small corner I occupy would be dark without my light. God must have put me here to be that light.

Without light, it would be impossible to appreciate most of God's creation. In fact, life as we know it would soon cease to be, without light. I wonder if God didn't pick the wrong metaphor. Such a vital function to be fulfilled by such inadequate creatures as myself! But I'm forgetting something. The same Lord who commanded "Let your light so shine" also said, "I am the light of the world" John 9:5b.

Prayer: God, Father of Lights; Jesus, Light of the

World; if I am to be light, please recharge my batteries. Become light in me, that others may see it, and give glory to You.

50. YOU ARE LIGHT

Scripture Reading: Matthew 5:14-16; John 9:5b

"Let your light so shine before men ..." Matt. 5:16, RSV.

"I am the light of the world" John 9:5b, RSV.

Forget the metaphors a minute and let's get practical. How can a mother be "light"? Sometimes it seems we really are tied to our homes. All right, so be it; how about a shift in mental attitude? Instead of thinking of our homes as a trap, let's think of them as a vehicle for transmitting light.*

I recently came across a statement by Karen Mains, a minister's wife in Chicago. "In this inhospitable world, a Christian home is a miracle to be shared." Maybe the light can be shared with Keith, who lives next door, and who always tracks dirt in the house, always seems hungry, and whose language I'd just as soon my children didn't pick up. Maybe the light could shine over to my recently widowed neighbor in the form of some companionship, or a meal, or some homemade rolls, or a listening ear. Maybe there are some college students who would welcome a place to

*Recommended Reading: *The Christian Family,* by Larry Christenson. Minneapolis: Bethany Fellowship, 1970.

kick off their shoes and raid the refrigerator. Maybe I could start a neighborhood Bible study.

Jesus didn't exempt mothers from the statement, "Let your light so shine." He expects us to shine from the location in which He has put us, our homes. He knows our energies are limited, and He knows that our homes are not perfect places—nonetheless, we have been commanded to let our lights shine. But Jesus reassures us with the fact that He, Himself, is our light!

51. THAT'S A NO, BUT HERE'S A YES

Scripture Reading: Genesis 2:8, 9, 15, 16, 17;
Exodus 20:2, 3; III John 11; I Peter 3:11

"The Lord God charged man: you may eat freely from every tree in the garden; but do not eat from the tree of knowing good and evil; for the day you eat from it you will cetrainly die" Gen. 2:16, 17, Berk.

"I AM THE LORD YOUR GOD! ... You shall have no other gods before My face" Exod. 20:2, 3, Berk.

"Do not imitate evil, but good" III John 11, Berk.

As parents, we sometimes have to say "no" to our children. This is right and necessary. But are we as quick to say "Yes"? With Kristin, whenever we had to say "no," we tried hard to find a "yes." The knife is a "no," but this wooden spoon is a "yes." Coloring on the wall is "no," but on this paper is a "yes." I was amazed, several years later, when big sister Kristin

74

pulled a dangerous object away from Emily, and said, "That's a no, but here's a yes!"

God has laid down certain "NOs" for His people: "Do NOT eat from the tree of knowing good and evil," "Have NO other gods before my face," "Do NOT imitate evil," etc. But the Church has, at times, been guilty of so emphasizing God's "NOs" that it has neglected to emphasize God's "YESses"—often found right together with the NOs! "Do NOT eat of the tree . . ."; but every other tree in the garden was a YES! "Have no other Gods . . ."; because I AM YOUR GOD! I am all you need. I am your YES! "Do not imitate evil . . ."; but do good. That is a Yes. Be so busy doing good you haven't time to do evil. Maybe some of us need to reorient our thinking. Have we been so busy teaching our children, "O Be Careful Little Feet Where You Go," that we have neglected to teach them to sing, "Take My Feet and Let Them Be Swift and Beautiful for Thee"? The "Thou shalt nots" are important; but our lives will be empty unless they are filled with "Thou shalts."

52. BUT, MOM...

Scripture Reading: Jonah 1-3

"The Word of the Lord came to Jonah . . . Get up and go to Nineveh . . . But Jonah arose to flee from the presence of the Lord" Jonah 1.

But, Mom, I'm just too tired to empty the waste-baskets . . . Mom, Raggedy Ann is sick, and I have to take care of her . . . tears . . . Why can't Emily empty the wastebaskets? . . . Mom, I have to help Jo, don't you think I ought to help Jo? . . . I'll do them tomorrow, Mom, why can't I do them tomorrow? . . . You're mean, Mom, to make me do all this hard work . . . tears. . .

It would really be easier to empty the wastebaskets myself. . .

Often our dealings with our children give us a clearer understanding of God's dealings with us. I wonder how God feels about the tasks He's assigned me! As I marvel at how many excuses a four-year-old can think up, I can't help but smile at how familiar they sound! Think of all the excuses and complaints God has had to listen to as His children go through the process of being sanctified! Yet the tasks He assigns, though challenging, are never too difficult. "God is reliable, who will not permit you to be tempted (tested) beyond your ability" (I Cor. 10:13, Berk.). God is not swayed by our excuses. His will is ultimately done (See Jonah). And God doesn't give up on His children. He is always standing by to help when that help is necessary. "Then Jonah prayed to the Lord his God from the belly of the fish and said, 'I called to the Lord out of my anguish, and He answered me. From the innermost part of Sheol I cried for help—Thou didst listen to my voice' " (Jonah 2:1, 2, Berk.).

Imperfectly as we do our tasks, and despite our complaints and excuses, God has chosen us, His children, to do the work of His Kingdom here on earth! And somehow, in the process, He is shaping us into the kind of people He wants us to become.

53. WALK IN MY SHOES

Scripture Reading: Colossians 3
"Follow my example, as I follow Christ's"
I Cor. 11:1, NEB.

Emily has always had a preoccupation with shoes—I wondered about it until it finally occurred to me that, much of the time, all she sees of the adult world is shoes! We all laughed the other day, when she trudged into the kitchen, wearing a pair of my shoes, very pleased at her accomplishment.

Our children very quickly learn to walk in our shoes, to talk our language, and to imitate our mannerisms. A friend of mine had a young child visiting her children. After her children had prayed, the child who was a guest wanted to say a prayer. But instead of concluding her prayer, "In Jesus' Name, Amen," she closed it with profanity—words, the meaning of which she may not even have known, but it was evident this was the context in which she was accustomed to hearing the names of God, or Jesus.

I admire Paul for being unafraid to say, "Imitate me, as I imitate Christ" (Berk.). As I see my children picking up my mannerisms, it scares me. I'm not sure I'm the best model. I wish that my children could already imitate Christ directly. In time I trust that they will, but for now they must be able to see Christ through my life.

Prayer: God, Help me keep my eyes on You! Too often I do such a poor job of walking in Your shoes. Help me, for the sake of the little ones who will get their first glimpse of You by seeing You in me.

54. A MOTHER'S PSALM OF THANKS

(Inspired by Psalm 136)

Scripture Reading: Psalm 136

Give thanks to the Lord, for He is good,
For His covenant love is everlasting.

Give thanks to the God of gods,
For His covenant love is everlasting.

He has put us here, in this country,
    this city, and this neighborhood.
For His covenant love is everlasting.

He has provided us a church family with which to
    worship,
For His covenant love is everlasting.

He has provided that my refrigerator and freezer
    are loaded with good things to eat.
For His covenant love is everlasting.

He has given us this house in which to live;
For His covenant love is everlasting.

He who knows me as He knows all things,
    has allowed me to live in this post-washing
    machine age!
For His covenant love is everlasting.

The beach, with its soft sand, warm sunshine,
    and cool water, is His creation.
For His covenant love is everlasting.

He allowed some of His creatures to discover how to
    use radiotherapy, so that Steve's Hodgkin's Dis-
    ease could be arrested.
For His covenant love is everlasting.

Each of the billions of snowflakes is a unique
expression of His unlimited creativity.
For His covenant love is everlasting.

See the stars in the clear night sky! He who put them
there in all their splendor, keeps them there.
For His covenant love is everlasting.

Look at this tomato, fresh from the garden. Its bright
red goodness is a treat for both eye and palate.
For His covenant love is everlasting.

After a difficult day, He gives sleep to my weary body.
For His covenant love is everlasting.

The warm winter coat I found on sale for Kristin;
that, too, is part of His provision.
For His covenant love is everlasting.

He has given my children strong, healthy bodies,
and keen minds.
For His covenant love is everlasting.

Even the baby cardinals, loudly announcing their
hunger from the nest in the tree outside, are
provided for.
For His covenant love is everlasting.

He performs daily miracles within my body,
as the child I carry develops and grows.
For His covenant love is everlasting.

He has provided me with some caring friends.
For His covenant love is everlasting.

He has made available to me and my family a remedy
for sin.
For His covenant love is everlasting.

Give thanks to the God of heaven.
For His covenant love is everlasting.

55. THE POTENTATE OF TIME

Scripture Reading: Ecclesiastes 3, Psalm 102:24-28

"But I trust in Thee, O Lord; I said, 'Thou art my God; my times are in Thy hand;'" Ps. 31:14, 15a, Berk.

> Crown Him the Lord of Years,
> The Potentate of Time;
> Creator of the rolling spheres
> Ineffably sublime
> All hail, Redeemer, hail!
> For thou hast died for me:
> Thy praise shall never, never fail
> Throughout eternity.
> —Matthew Bridges

LORD OF YESTERDAY:

Thank you, God, for many good yesterdays. You have given me a life enriched by the love of family and friends, and colored by many and varied experiences. There are some yesterdays when I made wrong choices; where I failed the people I love. I thank You for Your forgiveness, and that you are in control of those yesterdays, too.

LORD OF TODAY:

Today is the first day of the rest of eternity! Thank You that there is enough time today for the tasks You have in mind for me. If I find myself running short of time, help me to examine my tasks, and to determine which of them were my idea alone, not Yours.

LORD OF TOMORROW:

Thank You, Father, that I can approach tomorrow and the tomorrows that follow without fear or apprehension. Each day is a new opportunity to continue becoming the person You created me to be. You have a job for me to do here on earth, and when that has been completed—not a day too soon, or a day too late—You who are the Potentate of Time will release me from the bondage of Time.